Small Business Guide to FDA

Table of Contents

Introduction

The purpose of this guide is to help small businesses – usually those with fewer than 500 employees — successfully navigate the realm of regulatory measures with which he U.S. Food and Drug Administration (FDA or the Agency) protects and promotes the health of the American public.

Familiarity with FDA requirements is very important for a small firm that manufactures or plans to manufacture, sell, warehouse, transport, or import any of the thousands of FDA regulated products. To reach the U.S. interstate market, these products must comply with the applicable laws and the science-based public health rules developed and enforced by FDA.

Although this obligation is routinely fulfilled by hundreds of thousands of American businesses, FDA is aware that for a small firm it can present a challenge. The Agency's responsibilities are defined in some 200 federal laws, and the resulting requirements, which can be complex, cover hundreds of pages in the Code of Federal Regulations. To find their way in this extensive domain of requirements, small and start-up businesses are likely to need expert assistance.

The purpose of this guide is to help satisfy this need. Chapters I-IV provide an overview of FDA's responsibilities and operations and outline the main areas where small firms are most likely to come in contact with the Agency. Chapter V provides links to information that small businesses most frequently request from FDA's product centers and the Agency's Office of Regulatory Affairs. Chapter VI lists the Agency's offices and individuals who are ready to help small firms resolve their regulatory problems.

This guide is designed to help make the small firms' contacts with FDA as efficient and productive as possible. We present this document as a blueprint that firms can follow to achieve their business aims while helping FDA accomplish its public health mission.

Chapter I — FDA: the Big Picture

The first — and most basic — question that's often asked is this: why do some products and services have to be regulated?

FDA's regulations are designed to prevent, or at least minimize, health risks that began emerging more than a century ago when the production of food and medical products became industrialized, and could no longer be controlled by individual consumers. In 1901, there were no mandatory federal manufacturing or product standards for biologics. The deaths of 13 children in St. Louis in 1901 as a result of receiving tetanus-contaminated diphtheria antitoxin, and other similar incidents, prompted quick action by lawmakers. The Biologics Control Act (also called the Virus-Toxin Law) was passed on July 1, 1902, with little comment or publicity. The Act mandated annual licensing of establishments to manufacture and sell vaccines, sera, antitoxins, and similar product in interstate commerce. In 1906, after the country was shocked by an exposé of unhygienic conditions in the Chicago stockyards, Congress enacted the Food and Drugs Act prohibiting interstate commerce in misbranded and adulterated food, drugs and drinks. Enforcement of the Act, which made public health protection a federal responsibility, was entrusted to the U.S. Department of Agriculture's Bureau of Chemistry, which in 1930 became FDA.

Since then, Congress has repeatedly responded to new public health needs by expanding FDA's role and authority. In 1938, after a toxic elixir killed 107 people, Congress enacted the Food, Drug and Cosmetic Act. Among other provisions, the law authorized FDA to demand evidence of safety for new drugs, issue standards for food, and conduct factory inspections. In 1944 the Biologics Control Act of 1902 was incorporated into the Public Health Service (PHS) Act, which helped to define the shape of medical research after World War II. In 1962, the thalidomide tragedy in Europe inspired the Kefauver-Harris Amendments that required the proof of new drugs' effectiveness as well as safety. In 1976, following reports of thousands of injuries caused by faulty intrauterine devices (or IUDs), the Medical Device Amendments called for similar safeguards for medical devices. And in 2009, Congress took a major step to reduce the death toll of tobacco by passing the Family Smoking Prevention and Tobacco Control Act.

Today, congressional mandates shield Americans from a large number of public health hazards. The laws require FDA to ensure the safety of about 80 percent of the U.S. food supply — everything we eat except for meat, poultry and some egg products, which are regulated by USDA — and all dietary supplements and food additives.

Another major FDA responsibility is to ensure the safety and effectiveness of all drugs, biological agents including blood products and tissues for transplantation, and all medical devices.

In addition, FDA is required to evaluate the safety of animal drugs and feed; make sure that cosmetics and equipment that emits radiation do no harm; and, reduce the risks of the use of tobacco. Consumers spend about $1 trillion a year on these products, or about one-fifth of their total expenditures, but the protections offered by FDA cost each taxpayer less than one dollar a month.

FDA's wide-ranging and exacting activities are directed by a White House-appointed and U.S. Senate-confirmed Commissioner of Food and Drugs, and are carried out by the Agency's 13,500 employees, many of whom are health-care professionals and scientists. FDA operates seven centers. One of them — The National Center for Toxicological Research — performs studies that help provide the scientific base for FDA's regulations and reduce the potential health risks of regulated products. The other six centers are product-oriented, and their main responsibilities are as follows:

❖ **The Center for Food Safety and Applied Nutrition (CFSAN)** is charged with ensuring that food products and cosmetics do not contain hazardous contaminants, and that they are truthfully labeled.

❖ **The Center for Drug Evaluation and Research (CDER)** is a consumer watchdog in America's healthcare system. CDER's best-known job is to evaluate new drugs before they can be sold. The Center's review of new drug applications not only prevents quackery, but it provides doctors and patients with the information they need to use medicines wisely. CDER ensures that safe and effective drugs are available to improve the health of consumers, and that prescription and over-the-counter human drugs, both brand name and generic, work correctly and that the health benefits outweigh known risks.

❖ **The Center for Biologics Evaluation and Research (CBER)** works to ascertain the safety and effectiveness of biological products including vaccines, blood for transfusion and genes- cells- and tissues-based therapies, and helps defend the public against emerging infectious diseases and bioterrorism.

❖ **The Center for Devices and Radiological Health (CDRH)** is tasked with assuring the safety, effectiveness, and quality of medical devices, and ensuring the safety of radiation-emitting electronic products.

❖ **The Center for Veterinary Medicine (CVM)** regulates drugs, devices, and food additives given to, or used on, companion animals as well as poultry, cattle, swine and other animals used as food.

❖ **The Center for Tobacco Products (CTP)** regulates the manufacture, distribution, and marketing of tobacco products to protect public health. Some of CTP's responsibilities include setting performance standards, reviewing premarket applications for new and modified risk tobacco products, requiring new warning labels, and establishing and enforcing advertising and promotion restrictions.

In addition, about one-third of FDA employees are members of the Office of Regulatory Affairs (ORA) and are posted throughout the United States and abroad in regions that produce regulated products for export to the U.S. The mission of these specialists is to maximize compliance with FDA's product standards, minimize their risks, and enhance the public health.

Chapter II— Meeting FDA's Requirements

FDA's main responsibility is to help protect consumers against health hazards involving a broad range of products that include most of our food supply, all medications and medical devices, equipment that emits radiation, cosmetics, and numerous products for animals. The Agency performs this task by allowing these regulated products to be marketed across the state lines only if they meet science-based, rigorously defined public health standards and requirements.

The main responsibility of businesses that manufacture, distribute or import these products is to make sure that these requirements are met. For example:

❖ New human and veterinary drugs (those with new intended uses or new chemical ingredients) and medical devices (such as stair-climbing wheel chairs, contact lenses and heart pacemakers) must satisfy the Agency's science-based prerequisites for safety, quality and effectiveness, and their labeling must be accurate, thorough and not misleading.

❖ Substances added to food must comply with the standards of food additive regulations that are based on FDA's review of scientific evidence of their safety and utility.

❖ Drugs including medical gases, human and veterinary prescription drugs, over-the-counter (OTC) drugs, and certain biologics must register all establishments and list all drug products electronically.

❖ All domestic and foreign facilities that manufacture/process, pack, or hold food or feed and dietary supplements in the U.S. must register with FDA.

❖ Specific premarket controls apply to biological products that are required to be licensed under a federal law.

Small businesses that want to market these products or experiment with them in human or animal clinical trials have to file one or more applications with FDA and follow certain procedures. Although some regulated products (such as cosmetics, veterinary medical devices, and certain radiation-emitting equipment) do not need FDA's premarket approval, the Agency has the jurisdiction over standards and regulations that are applicable to their manufacture.

*(To ask for FDA's help in complying with the Agency's requirements, see **Chapter VI** for a complete list of sources that can assist small businesses in resolving regulatory problems.)*

Chapter III — Working With FDA

All firms in FDA's regulatory purview are affected by policies and regulations developed by the Agency to protect and promote the public health. These rules and policies can have considerable impact on small as well as large commercial establishments, but they are not created arbitrarily or in a vacuum. The Agency establishes them in a dialogue with its stakeholders that enables the affected firms to present their views and facts and influence the Agency's decisions. This chapter discusses the main forms of this dialogue and the ways in which the regulated firms can make their voices heard.

Comments on Rule Proposals

FDA routinely responds to a new legislative mandate or public health need by proposing a regulatory rule and publishing it in the *Federal Register (FR)*. These proposals describe the Agency's reasons for the proposed action and invite all stakeholders, including the regulated firms, to evaluate the proposed measure and comment on it by presenting their own facts or alternative approaches.

The Agency facilitates this dialogue in two ways: frequently, it precedes the formal proposal by publishing in the *FR* a "Notice of Intent" that announces the Agency's intention to consider the issue and that can be commented on by stakeholders. And routinely, the published proposal specifies a time period, usually of 60 days or more, during which all interested parties can supply their written comments — by mail, electronically or in person — to a special docket (or file) established by the Agency. Issues open to public comment often are reported by the news media and can be found at www.regulations.gov, a government website, with a search engine, and a wealth of information about rulemaking.

Each comment received by the Agency is logged, numbered, and placed in a file for that docket. It then becomes a public record and is available for anyone to examine at www.regulations.gov or in FDA Dockets Management's reading room (Room 1061, 5630 Fishers Lane, Rockville, MD 20852.). If FDA extends the period, a notice of the extension is published in the *FR*. Occasionally, the comments received may prompt the Agency to publish a second or third proposal addressing the same issue. Each substantive revision or amendment of an FDA proposal is announced in the *FR*.

FDA carefully studies all of the submitted views and information before issuing the final rule, which frequently incorporates some of the comments. The final regulation, which has the force of law, is published in the *FR* together with the Agency's responses to the received comments.

Other Opportunities for a Dialogue

FDA maintains a continuous dialogue with its stakeholders by holding public meetings, hearings and conferences, and by consulting with its advisory committees and panels of outside experts. These exchanges are usually of greatest interest to industry representatives or consumer groups but anyone can attend them and, with advance notice, comment on the discussed issue. FDA's public meetings are announced in the *FR* and most of them are held in the Washington, D.C. area.

Chapter IV: FDA Inspections and Product Recalls

Inspections

FDA may conduct a facility inspection for a variety of reasons, including a routinely scheduled investigation, a survey, or a response to a reported problem with a regulated product. Upon arrival, the FDA investigator presents his/her credentials and "Notice of Inspection" (FDA Form 482), and should be joined by a previously designated knowledgeable person, such as the plant or production manager. The firm's representative should accompany the investigator throughout the visit and ask questions if in doubt about the investigator's procedures.

Usually, the investigator will examine the production process, check certain records and collect samples. At the conclusion of the inspection, the FDA employee will discuss with the firm's management any significant findings and concerns, and produce a written report of any conditions or practices that the investigator considers objectionable.

This list of "Inspectional Observations," also called an FDA Form 483, usually does not recommend specific corrective measures, but can be used by the firm as a guide for the necessary improvements. The firm's manager(s) can and should respond to the reported observations during the discussion with the investigator. Corrective actions or procedural changes promptly taken in the presence of the investigator are regarded as indications of the firm's readiness to correct the reported deficiencies.

Concerns about the professional demeanor of any FDA employee during an inspection or the performance of other official duties should be reported to the nearest FDA district director listed in Chapter VI of this guide and at http://www.fda.gov/ICECI/Inspections/IOM/ ucm124008.htm. Objections to FDA's actions and questions about the Agency's jurisdiction should be presented to the ombudsman of the appropriate FDA product center (for address, see http://www.fda.gov/AboutFDA/ContactFDA/ResolveaDispute/HowtoContactanOmbuds man/CenterOmbudsmen/) or to:
FDA Office of the Ombudsman,
10903 New Hampshire Avenue
WO 32, Room 4231
Silver Spring, MD 20993
phone: 301-796-8530; fax: 301-847-8628;
e-mail: ombuds@oc.fda.gov.

Product Recalls

A "recall" is a firm's removal or correction of a marketed product that FDA considers to be in violation of the laws it administers and against which FDA would initiate a regulatory action such as a seizure of the product. During a recall, a firm can expect to work more closely with FDA than under almost any other circumstance. The first FDA official to be contacted by the manufacturer or distributor of the product to be recalled is the nearest FDA district recall coordinator listed at http://www.fda.gov/Safety/Recalls/IndustryGuidance/ucm129334.htm.

FDA's main concerns during a recall are that the firm knows the location of the suspected lots of the product and has organized their prompt removal from commerce. FDA will work with the firm to identify the cause of the problem and the corrections needed to prevent its recurrence.

The Agency is also concerned about the final disposition of the recalled products. This can be done by their destruction with appropriate regard for local laws concerning waste removal or incineration; by their reconditioning (relabeling, repacking, reworking, etc.); or, if permitted, by exportation. Any disposition must first be discussed with the FDA district office, because the Agency may wish to witness the effort. The recalling firm must maintain proper documentation of its actions.

In the case of device recalls, the firm must report to the FDA district office any product corrections or removals in accordance with 21 CFR 806.10 as soon as the firm becomes aware of the problem.

Essentially, the procedures for a product recall are determined by the individual company; however, a proper recall system should include provisions for record-keeping, handling of product returns, liaison with FDA, and public information. The efficiency of tracking and removing a product depends on the completeness of the records maintained throughout the production and distribution process.

Information on recalls of FDA regulated products is available online at www.fda.gov/Safety/Recalls.

Chapter V: Answers to Small Business FAQs

Center for Food Safety and Applied Nutrition (CFSAN)

The Center for Food Safety and Applied Nutrition (CFSAN), working together with FDA's field staff, is responsible for ensuring that the nation's food supply (everything we eat except for meat, poultry and some egg products that are regulated by the U.S. Department of Agriculture) is safe, sanitary, wholesome, and honestly labeled, and that cosmetic products are safe and properly labeled.

Small businesses can request CFSAN information by e-mailing their questions to industry@fda.gov or calling 1-888-SAFEFOOD or 1-888-723-3366.

Additional helpful information is posted on the following FDA websites:

- Manufactured Food Regulatory Program Standards:
  http://www.fda.gov/downloads/RegulatoryInformation/Guidances/UCM125448.pdf

- Registration of food facilities:
  http://www.fda.gov/food/guidancecomplianceregulatoryinformation/registrationoffoodfacilities/default.htm

- Establishment and maintenance of required records:
  http://www.fda.gov/Food/FoodDefense/Bioterrorism/Recordkeeping/ucm061619.htm

- FAQs on establishment and maintenance of records:
  http://www.fda.gov/Food/GuidanceComplianceRegulatoryInformation/GuidanceDocuments/FoodDefenseandEmergencyResponse/ucm062801.htm.

- Food security:
  http://www.fda.gov/Food/FoodDefense/default.htm.

- Regulatory compliance manual:
  http://www.fda.gov/ICECI/ComplianceManuals/ComplianceProgramManual/default.htm#Foods

- Inspections manual:
  http://www.fda.gov/ICECI/Inspections/IOM/default.htm

- Standards of food identity:
  http://www.accessdata.fda.gov/scripts/cdrh/cfdocs/cfcfr/cfrsearch.cfm.

- Food labeling requirements:
  http://www.fda.gov/Food/GuidanceComplianceRegulatoryInformation/GuidanceDocuments/FoodLabelingNutrition/default.htm

- Labeling of food allergens:
  http://www.fda.gov/Food/LabelingNutrition/FoodAllergensLabeling/GuidanceComplianceRegulatoryInformation/ucm2006884.htm

- Low-acid canned and acidified food requirements:
  http://www.fda.gov/Food/FoodSafety/Product-SpecificInformation/AcidifiedLow-AcidCannedFoods/default.htm

- Bottled water products:
  http://www.fda.gov/Food/FoodSafety/Product-SpecificInformation/BottledWaterCarbonatedSoftDrinks/default.htm

- HACCP requirements for juice products:
  http://www.fda.gov/Food/FoodSafety/HazardAnalysisCriticalControlPointsHACCP/JuiceHACCP/default.htm.

- HACCP requirements for seafood products:
  http://www.fda.gov/Food/GuidanceComplianceRegulatoryInformation/GuidanceDocuments/Seafood/FishandFisheriesProductsHazardsandControlsGuide/default.htm.

- Levels of unavoidable natural defects in food:
  http://www.fda.gov/Food/GuidanceComplianceRegulatoryInformation/GuidanceDocu
  ments/Sanitation/ucm056174.htm

- Poisonous and deleterious substances:
  http://www.fda.gov/Food/GuidanceComplianceRegulatoryInformation/GuidanceDocu
  ments/ChemicalContaminantsandPesticides/ucm077969.htm.

- Prior notice of imported food:
  http://www.fda.gov/Food/GuidanceComplianceRegulatoryInformation/PriorNoticeofI
  mportedFoods/default.htm

- The import process:
  http://www.fda.gov/ForIndustry/ImportProgram/default.htm.

- Information for cosmetics manufacturers, packagers and distributors:
  http://www.fda.gov/Cosmetics/ResourcesForYou/CosmeticsManufacturersPackagersD
  istributors/default.htm

- The Food Safety Modernization Act:
  http://www.fda.gov/Food/FoodSafety/FSMA/default.htm

- Link to Title 21 – Manufacturers should review Part 110 on Good Manufacturing
  Practices:
  http://www.accessdata.fda.gov/scripts/cdrh/cfdocs/cfCFR/CFRSearch.cfm

Center for Drug Evaluation and Research (CDER)

The Center for Drug Evaluation and Research (CDER) performs an essential public health task by making sure that safe and effective drugs are available to improve the health of people in the United States. The Center regulates over-the-counter and prescription drugs, including biological therapeutics and generic drugs. CDER's principal functions are to review the evidence that drugs are safe and effective before allowing them to be marketed; monitor their use for unexpected health risks; ensure their continued high quality; and oversee the accuracy and completeness of drug information provided for health professionals and consumers. The Center also conducts its own and collaborative drug-focused laboratory research and testing. However, the drug sponsors, not CDER, are responsible for conducting clinical trials.

CDER's numerous information resources for small firms include the following:

- Small Business Assistance website:
   http://www.fda.gov/smallbusinessdrugs supports the CDER Small Business Assistance Program's mission of promoting productive interaction with regulated industry by assisting regulated domestic and international small pharmaceutical business seeking timely and accurate information relating to development and regulation of human drug products. It provides information, among other topics, about drug development and review processes, FDA-related laws, regulations and guidances, information about FDA regulatory submissions, and economic incentives. It also posts information about CDER Small Business Assistance Program's outreach programs, such as workshops, webinars, CDERLearn, and email notifications.

- The Office of Communications, Division of Drug Information (DDI): www.fda.gov/aboutDDI is staffed by health care professionals who provide expert advice and guidance on all aspects of CDER activities.

- The Office of New Drugs (OND) contacts: http://www.fda.gov/downloads/AboutFDA/CentersOffices/CDER/UCM206032.pdf lists the names and phone numbers of OND's experts in therapeutic and product areas ranging from addiction to vitamins.

- CDER Guidance Documents: http://www.fda.gov/Drugs/GuidanceComplianceRegulatoryInformation/Guidances/default.htm represent the Agency's current thinking on a particular subject. They do not create or confer any rights for or on any person and do not operate to bind FDA or the public. The guidance documents cover numerous subjects including drug advertising, biopharmaceuticals, combination products, drug labeling and drug user fees.

- Regulatory information on over-the-counter (OTC) products at http://www.fda.gov/AboutFDA/CentersOffices/CDER/ucm106368.htm includes the list of FDA regulations open for comments, index of human OTC drug information published in the *Federal Register*, and the status of OTC rulemakings.

- The Code of Federal Regulations Part 21 http://www.accessdata.fda.gov/scripts/cdrh/cfdocs/cfcfr/CFRSearch.cfm covers the general enforcement rules including the product jurisdiction, organization and enforcement policy.

- FDA's Import program for pharmaceuticals http://www.fda.gov/ForIndustry/ImportProgram/default.htm includes all related subjects such as rules and data on import alerts, import refusals and import for export.

- The Export and Export Certificate website http://www.fda.gov/InternationalPrograms/ExportsandExportCertificates/default.htm informs on when it is permissible to export an unapproved, adulterated or misbranded product, and contains links to related FDA guidance documents and other resources.

- The National Drug Code directory http://www.fda.gov/Drugs/InformationOnDrugs/ucm142438.htm is updated twice a month and includes the list of all FDA-registered drug manufacturers, their products, and their identification numbers.

- The Orange Book http://www.fda.gov/Drugs/InformationOnDrugs/ucm129662.htm allows you to search for official information about FDA approved drug products, and contains information about therapeutic equivalence, evaluations and drug patents and exclusivity.

- Drugs@FDA http://www.accessdata.fda.gov/scripts/cder/drugsatfda allows you to search for official information about FDA approved brand name and generic drugs and therapeutic biological products.

Center for Biologics Evaluation and Research (CBER)

The Center for Biologics Evaluation and Research (CBER) protects and advances the public health by ensuring that biological products are safe, effective and available to those who need them. Biologics include a wide range of products such as vaccines, blood and blood components, allergenics, and cell, tissue and gene therapies. These products are isolated from natural sources — human, animal or microorganism — and are often produced by cutting-edge technologies.

CBER's main web page for information for industry is:
http://www.fda.gov/BiologicsBloodVaccines/ResourcesforYou/Industry/default.htm.

The following links provide information on topics most often inquired about by small businesses:

Biologics Regulations and General Information

- Title 21 parts 600 to 680 contain key manufacturing regulations specific to biological products. In addition the drug or device regulations are also applicable to biological products.

- The text of key 21 CFR regulations at http://www.accessdata.fda.gov/scripts/cdrh/cfdocs/cfcfr/CFRSearch.cfm cover the general enforcement rules including the product jurisdiction, organization and enforcement policy.

- Guidance, compliance and regulatory information are posted at: http://www.fda.gov/BiologicsBloodVaccines/GuidanceComplianceRegulatoryInformation/default.htm.

Tissue and Tissue Products

- Main webpage: http://www.fda.gov/BiologicsBloodVaccines/TissueTissueProducts/default.htm

- Information about donor eligibility, establishment registration, and tissue products: http://www.fda.gov/BiologicsBloodVaccines/TissueTissueProducts/QuestionsaboutTissues/ucm101559.htm

- Related link to frequently asked questions about tissue and tissue products: www.fda.gov/BiologicsBloodVaccines/TissueTissueProducts/QuestionsaboutTissues/ucm101559.htm

- Guidance for Tissue Donor Eligibility Determination: http://www.fda.gov/BiologicsBloodVaccines/GuidanceComplianceRegulatoryInformation/Guidances/Tissue/ucm073964.htm.

- For CBER's Compliance Program Guidance Manual on Inspection of Human Cells, Tissues, and Cellular and Tissue-Based Products (HCT/Ps) 7341.002, see: http://www.fda.gov/downloads/BiologicsBloodVaccines/GuidanceComplianceRegulatoryInformation/ComplianceActivities/Enforcement/CompliancePrograms/UCM095216.pdf.

- HCT/Ps regulated under 351 PHS Act are also subject to applicable regulations in 21 CFR 1271 and are described at: http://www.accessdata.fda.gov/scripts/cdrh/cfdocs/cfcfr/CFRSearch.cfm?CFRPart=1271.

Biologic Product Deviation Reporting (BPDR)

- General instructions for completing form FDA 3486 are at: http://www.fda.gov/BiologicsBloodVaccines/SafetyAvailability/ReportaProblem/BiologicalProductDeviations/ucm129716.htm.

- There are also instructions for use of eBPDR system at: http://www.fda.gov/BiologicsBloodVaccines/SafetyAvailability/ReportaProblem/BiologicalProductDeviations/ucm134535.htm.

- CBER's web page on reporting of HCT/P deviation at: http://www.fda.gov/BiologicsBloodVaccines/SafetyAvailability/ReportaProblem/BiologicalProductDeviations/default.htm includes links to forms and instructions for such actions as completing and electronically submitting the Biological Product Deviation Report (BPDR) and to Biological Product Deviation Guidances and Rules.

- CBER BPDR page is located at: http://www.fda.gov/BiologicsBloodVaccines/SafetyAvailability/ReportaProblem/BiologicalProductDeviations/ucm129804.htm.

- Inquiries pertaining to BPDR for blood and blood products or HCT/Ps can be sent to bp_deviations@fda.hhs.gov or hctp_deviations@fda.hhs.gov , respectively.

Establishment Registration

- Information about human cell and tissue establishment registration for registered, inactive and pre-registered firms is located at: http://www.fda.gov/BiologicsBloodVaccines/GuidanceComplianceRegulatoryInformation/EstablishmentRegistration/TissueEstablishmentRegistration/ucm148002.htm.

- Tissue Registration page for directions on how to register is at: http://www.fda.gov/BiologicsBloodVaccines/GuidanceComplianceRegulatoryInformation/EstablishmentRegistration/TissueEstablishmentRegistration/default.htm. Questions about registration information can be emailed to the Tissue Registration Coordinator at tissuereg@fda.hhs.gov.

- Blood establishment registration and product listing has a webpage for contact on blood establishment registration and product listing: http://www.accessdata.fda.gov/scripts/email/cber/bldregcontact.cfm. There is an email address at bloodregis@fda.hhs.gov for submitting blood registration questions.

- Plasma Center Establishments can be registered electronically at: http://www.fda.gov/BiologicsBloodVaccines/GuidanceComplianceRegulatoryInformation/EstablishmentRegistration/BloodEstablishmentRegistration/default.htm

Investigational New Drug Applications

- Information on submitting to CBER an Investigation New Drug (IND) Application is posted at:
- http://www.fda.gov/BiologicsBloodVaccines/DevelopmentApprovalProcess/InvestigationalNewDrugINDorDeviceExemptionIDEProcess/ucm094309.htm.

- The CBER IND or device exemption process is described on the FDA website: http://www.fda.gov/BiologicsBloodVaccines/DevelopmentApprovalProcess/InvestigationalNewDrugINDorDeviceExemptionIDEProcess/default.htm

- See this site for the IND form: http://www.fda.gov/AboutFDA/ReportsManualsForms/Forms/default.htm.

- Frequently asked questions about statement of investigator (FDA Form 1572) and May 2010 information sheet guidance are located at: http://www.fda.gov/downloads/RegulatoryInformation/Guidances/UCM214282.pdf.

- FDA form 1572 statement of investigator is available at: http://www.fda.gov/AboutFDA/CentersOffices/CDER/ucm090301.htm .

Center for Devices and Radiological Health (CDRH)

FDA's Center for Devices and Radiological Health (CDRH) is responsible for regulating firms that manufacture, repackage, relabel, and/or import medical devices sold in the United States. CDRH also regulates radiation-emitting electronic products (medical and non-medical) such as lasers, x-ray systems, ultrasound equipment, and microwave ovens.

Basic information and advice for small device companies is available at the following websites:

- Device Advice: Device Regulation and Guidance:
  The website of the CDRH Division of Small Manufacturers, International and Consumer Assistance (DSMICA) website (http://www.fda.gov/MedicalDevices/DeviceRegulationandGuidance/ucm142656.htm) provides technical and regulatory assistance to small manufacturers to help them comply with FDA requirements for medical devices.

- FDA Basics - Medical Devices:
  http://www.fda.gov/AboutFDA/Transparency/Basics/ucm193731.htm
  explains what medical devices are and how FDA regulates them.

- Frequently Asked Questions (FAQs) at http://www.fda.gov/AboutFDA/Transparency/Basics/ucm193731.htm address medical device basics; the device review process; information about devices; and device safety.

- CDRH Learn:
  http://www.fda.gov/Training/CDRHLearn/default.htm consists of training modules that describe premarket and postmarket aspects of medical device and radiological health regulation. Many of the modules are available in English, Chinese and Spanish.

- Twitter:
  Information about CDRH and medical devices is also communicated by Twitter located at @FDADeviceInfo and @FDAcdrhIndustry.

FDA has classified medical devices into Class I, II and III. Classification is based upon the controls deemed necessary to protect public health. Regulatory control increases from Class I to III. Most Class I devices are exempt from Premarket Notification [510(k)]; Class II devices require 510(k); and Class III devices require Premarket Approval (PMA). A description of device classification and a link to the Product Classification Database are available at http://www.fda.gov/MedicalDevices/DeviceRegulationandGuidance/Overview/ClassifyYourDevice/default.htm

Information about the basic regulatory requirements for medical device manufacturers is posted at the following websites:

- Establishment registration and medical device listing:
  http://www.fda.gov/MedicalDevices/DeviceRegulationandGuidance/GuidanceDocuments/ucm185871.htm

- Premarket Notification 510(k), unless exempt, or Premarket Approval (PMA):
  o http://www.fda.gov/MedicalDevices/DeviceRegulationandGuidance/HowtoMarketYourDevice/PremarketSubmissions/PremarketNotification510k/default.htm

  o http://www.fda.gov/MedicalDevices/DeviceRegulationandGuidance/HowtoMarketYourDevice/PremarketSubmissions/PremarketApprovalPMA/default.htm

- Investigational Device Exemption (IDE) for clinical studies:
  http://www.fda.gov/MedicalDevices/DeviceRegulationandGuidance/HowtoMarketYourDevice/InvestigationalDeviceExemptionIDE/default.htm

- Quality System (QS) regulation:
  http://www.fda.gov/MedicalDevices/DeviceRegulationandGuidance/PostmarketRequirements/QualitySystemsRegulations/default.htm

- Labeling requirements:
  http://www.fda.gov/MedicalDevices/DeviceRegulationandGuidance/Overview/DeviceLabeling/default.htm

- Medical Device Reporting (MDR):
  http://www.fda.gov/MedicalDevices/Safety/ReportaProblem/default.htm

Center for Veterinary Medicine (CVM)

The Center for Veterinary Medicine (CVM) regulates the manufacture and distribution of food additives, drugs and devices given to, or used on, pets, and animals from which human foods are derived. These animals include more than one hundred million companion animals, plus millions of poultry, cattle, swine, and minor animal species. (Minor animal species are animals other than cattle, swine, chickens, turkeys, horses, dogs, and cats.)

You can contact CVM by e-mail at AskCVM@fda.hhs.gov or Industry.AnimalVeterinary@fda.gov or by calling 240-276-9300. We also post information about CVM activities on Twitter at @FDAAnimalhealth

The following links provide CVM's responses to questions frequently asked by small businesses:

- How FDA regulates veterinary devices:
  http://www.fda.gov/AnimalVeterinary/ResourcesforYou/ucm047117.htm

- FDA Information about Animal Food and Feeds:
  http://www.fda.gov/AnimalVeterinary/Products/AnimalFoodFeeds/default.htm

- FDA information about the manufacture of pet food and pet treats:
  o http://www.fda.gov/AnimalVeterinary/Products/AnimalFoodFeeds/PetFood/default.htm

  o http://www.fda.gov/AnimalVeterinary/NewsEvents/FDAVeterinarianNewsletter/ucm093741.htm

- New Animal Drug Application process:
  o http://www.fda.gov/AnimalVeterinary/ResourcesforYou/AnimalHealthLiteracy/ucm219207.htm

  o http://www.fda.gov/AnimalVeterinary/DevelopmentApprovalProcess/default.htm

- Generic Animal Drug Approval process:
  http://www.fda.gov/AnimalVeterinary/GuidanceComplianceEnforcement/ActsRulesRegulations/ucm049100.htm

- Procedures for submitting a feed additive petition:
  http://www.fda.gov/AnimalVeterinary/DevelopmentApprovalProcess/ucm056809.htm

- Animal Drugs @ FDA (CVM's database of approved animal drugs):
  http://www.accessdata.fda.gov/scripts/animaldrugsatfda/

Center for Tobacco Products (CTP)

The Center for Tobacco Products (CTP) oversees the implementation of the Family Smoking Prevention and Tobacco Control Act (TCA), which added Chapter IX to the Federal Food, Drug, and Cosmetic Act (FD&C Act). It gives FDA the authority to regulate the manufacture, distribution, and marketing of tobacco products to protect public health. Some of CTP's responsibilities under the law include setting performance standards, reviewing premarket applications for new and modified risk tobacco products, requiring new warning labels, and establishing and enforcing advertising, marketing, and promotion restrictions.

CTP's Office of Small Business Assistance (OSBA) was established pursuant to section 901(f) of the FD&C Act. OSBA is charged with providing technical and other nonfinancial assistance to small tobacco product manufacturers to assist them in complying with the requirements of the TCA. In addition to manufacturers, OSBA provides support to other small tobacco businesses. OSBA assists these businesses through content on CTP's website, by hosting webinars, and responding to inquiries through CTP's Call Center and e-mail.

CTP's "For Industry" webpage (www.fda.gov/TobaccoProducts/ResourcesforYou/ ForIndustry/default.htm) provides tobacco businesses with news, information, and educational materials to help them comply with the TCA. From the "For Industry" webpage, you can link to OSBA's webpage where you will find additional information relevant to small businesses. Additionally, you can sign up for alerts to receive updated news and information related to tobacco regulation. There is also information on how to contact CTP for further information.

If you would like additional assistance, you can contact CTP at 1-877-CTP-1373 or AskCTP@fda.hhs.gov.

Office of Regulatory Affairs (ORA)

FDA's Office of Regulatory Affairs provides leadership for all FDA field activities and policies involving imports, inspections and enforcement. ORA supports the FDA product centers by inspecting regulated products and manufacturers, conducting sample analysis on regulated products, and reviewing imported products offered for entry into the United States. ORA also develops FDA-wide policy on compliance and enforcement and executes FDA's import strategy and food protection plans.

Some ORA experts are posted in FDA's offices in China, India, Latin America and Europe, but most of ORA's 3,575 employees are dispersed throughout the United States, including Washington, D.C., the U.S. Virgin Islands, Puerto Rico and all states except for Wyoming. Over 85 percent of ORA's staff works in 5 regional offices, 20 district offices, 13 laboratories, and more than 150 resident posts and border stations. Chapter VI of this guide includes a complete list of regional and district offices and ORA's small business representatives.

Because ORA's activities involve FDA-regulated products, many regulatory questions raised by industry are addressed by the appropriate centers and are discussed on the preceding pages of this guide. In addition, ORA is frequently asked to provide small firms with the following information:

- **FDA's Freedom of Information procedures** are described in FDA Staff Manual Guides, Volume III, located at: http://www.fda.gov/AboutFDA/ReportsManualsForms/StaffManualGuides/ucm138408.htm

- **Instructions for filing requests for FOI information** are available at: http://www.fda.gov/AboutFDA/ReportsManualsForms/StaffManualGuides/ucm138408.htm#7.%20Requests%20and%20Records%20Subject%20to%20FOI

- **FDA's inspection process** is covered in FDA's Investigations Operations Manual, Chapter 5, "Establishment Inspections" posted at:
  http://www.fda.gov/ICECI/Inspections/IOM/ucm123287.htm

- **Procedures for releasing FDA's Establishment Inspection Records** are described at:
  http://www.fda.gov/ICECI/Inspections/FieldManagementDirectives/ucm103299.htm

- **Management of operation involving a product recall** is discussed at:
  http://www.fda.gov/ICECI/Inspections/FieldManagementDirectives/ucm096029.htm

- **FDA's import program overview, import alerts and import operations** are outlined at:
  http://www.fda.gov/forindustry/importprogram/default.htm.

Office of Special Health Issues (OSHI)

- The MedWatch program:
  www.fda.gov/safety/MedWatch promotes the safe use of regulated products by rapidly disseminating new safety information and encouraging voluntary reporting of serious adverse events, product quality problems, medication errors and other unexpected health hazards associated with the use of regulated products.

Chapter VI: Helpful Contacts

General Assistance

Small companies seeking FDA's assistance and information should direct their first inquiries to the following resources:

Main FDA address and phone number (for general inquiries):

U.S. Food and Drug Administration
10903 New Hampshire Ave.
Silver Spring, MD 20993
1-888-INFO-FDA (1-888-463-6332)

FDA's Small Business Representatives (SBRs):

SBRs respond to small business inquiries, conduct or participate in workshops and conferences, and can visit business facilities to provide assistance.

Northeast Region
serving CT, MA, ME, NH, NY, RI, VT
(HFR-NEl7) Marilyn Rodriguez-Bohorquez
158-15 Liberty Avenue
Jamaica, NY 11433-1034
Phone (718) 662-5618

FAX (718) 662-5434
marilyn.bohorquez@fda.hhs.gov

Southwest Region
serving AR, CO, IA, KS, MO, NE, NM, OK, TX, UT, WY, US-Mexico Border Imports
(HFR-SW17) David Arvelo
4040 N. Central Expressway, Suite 900
Dallas, TX 75204
Phone (214) 253-4952
FAX (214) 253-4970
david.arvelo@fda.hhs.gov

Assistance on the Internet:

These sites explain how FDA laws and regulations apply to various products or specific circumstances and suggest methods for meeting these requirements.

- Drugs (CDER)
  http://www.fda.gov/smallbusinessdrugs

- Foods, dietary supplements and cosmetics (CFSAN)
  http://www.fda.gov/Food/ResourcesForYou/FoodIndustry/

- Medical devices (DSMICA in CDRH)
  o http://www.fda.gov/MedicalDevices/DeviceRegulationandGuidance/ucm142656.htm
  or
  o http://www.fda.gov/MedicalDevices/DeviceRegulationandGuidance/

- Biologics (CBER)
  http://www.fda.gov/BiologicsBloodVaccines/ResourcesforYou/Industry/

- Animal products (CVM)
  http://www.fda.gov/AnimalVeterinary/

FDA speaker requests for industry meetings and conferences:

Food and Drug Administration
Office of External Relations
Program and Speaker Coordination Staff
10903 New Hampshire Avenue
Silver Spring, MD 20203
Kenneth.Nolan@fda.hhs.gov

FDA Regional and District Offices

Northeast region:

New York Regional Office
Gail T. Costello, director
158-15 Liberty Avenue
Jamaica, NY 11433-1034
Phone - (718) 662-5416
FAX - (718) 662-5434
Area served: CT, MA, ME, NH, NY, RI, VT

New York District Office
Otto D. Vitillo, director
158-15 Liberty Avenue
Jamaica, N.Y. 11433-1034
Phone - (7l8) 662-5447
FAX - (718) 662-5665
Area served: NY

New England District Office
John Marzilli, director
One Montvale Ave.
Stoneham, MA 02180
Phone - (78l) 596-7717
FAX - (78l) 596-7896
Area served: CT, MA, ME, NH, RI, VT

Central region:

Philadelphia Regional Office
Melinda K. Plaiser, director
U.S. Customhouse
200 Chestnut St., Room 900
Philadelphia, PA 19106
Phone - (2l5) 597-4390
FAX - (215) 597-5798
Area served: Washington DC, DE, IL, IN,
KY, MD, MI, MN, ND, NJ, OH, PA, SD, VA,
WI, WV

Philadelphia District Office
Kirk Sooter, director
U.S. Customhouse
2nd and Chestnut Sts., Room 900
Philadelphia, PA 19106
Phone - (215) 597-4390
FAX - (215) 597-4660
Area served: DE, PA

Chicago District Office
Scott J. MacIntire, director
550 W. Jackson Blvd.
Suite 1500 South
Chicago, IL 60661
Phone - (312) 353-5863
FAX - (312) 596-4187
Area served: IL

Baltimore District Office
Evelyn Bonnin, director
6000 Metro Dr. Suite 101
Baltimore, MD 21215
Phone - (410) 779-5454
FAX - (410) 779-5707
Area served: Washington DC, MD, VA, WV

Cincinnati District Office
Teresa C. Thompson, director
6751 Steger Drive
Cincinnati, OH 45237-3097
Phone - (513) 679-2700
FAX - (513) 679-2771
Area served: KY, OH

New Jersey District Office
Diana Amador, director
Waterview Corporate Center
10 Waterview Blvd., 3rd Floor
Parsippany, NJ 07054
Phone - (973) 526-6000
FAX - (973) 526-6069
Area served: NJ

Detroit District Office
Joann M. Givens, director
300 River Place Drive
Suite 5900
Detroit, MI 48207-4457
Phone - (313) 393-8100
FAX - (313) 393-8105
Area served: IN, MI

Minneapolis District Office
Director: vacant
212 3rd Ave., South
Minneapolis, MN 55401-2532
Phone - (612) 334-4100

FAX - (612) 334-4134
Area served: MN, ND, SD, WI

Southeast region:

Atlanta Regional Office
Malcolm Frazier, director
60 Eighth St. N.E.
Atlanta, GA 30309
Phone - (404) 253-1171
FAX - (404) 253-1207
Area served: AL, FL, GA, LA, MS, NC, PR,
SC, TN, VI

Atlanta District Office
John Gridley, director
60 Eighth St. N.E.
Atlanta, GA 30309
Phone - (404) 253-1161
FAX - (404) 253-1202
Area served: GA, NC, SC

New Orleans District Office
H. Tyler Thornburg, director
404 BNA Dr Blg 200 Ste 500
Nashville, TN 37217
Phone - (615) 366-7801
FAX - (615) 366-7802
Area served: AL, LA, MS, TN

Florida District Office
Emma R. Singleton, director
555 Winderly Place. Suite 200
Maitland, FL 32751
Phone - (407) 253-1161
FAX - (407) 253-1202
Area served: FL

San Juan District Office
Maridalia Torres Irizarry, director
466 Fernandez Juncos Avenue
San Juan, PR 00901-3223
Phone - (787) 474-9500
FAX - (787) 729-6851
Area served: PR, VI

Southwest region:

Dallas Regional Office
Dennis Baker, director
4040 N. Central Expressway, Suite 900
Dallas, TX 75204
Phone - (214) 253-4901

FAX - (214) 253-4960
Area served: AR, CO, IA, KS, MO, NE, NM,
OK, TX, UT, WY, US-Mexico Border
Imports

Dallas District Office
Reynaldo (Ricky) R. Rodriguez, Jr.
4040 N. Central Expressway, Suite 300
Dallas, TX 75204
Phone - (214) 253-5200
FAX - (214) 253-5313
Area served: AR, OK, TX

Southwest Import District
Todd Cato, director
4040 N. Central Expressway, Suite 300
Dallas, TX 75204
Phone - (214) 253-5330
Toll-free - (800) 991-4881
FAX - (214) 253-5316
Area served: AR, AZ, CA, CO, IA, KS, MO,
NE, NM, OK, TX, UT, WY, US-Mexico
border imports

Denver District Office
Harry T. Warwick, director
6th & Kipling Sts., Denver Federal Ctr
Bldg. 20, Entrance W-l0
Denver, CO 80225-0087
Phone - (303) 236-3000
FAX - (303) 236-3099
(Mailing Address:
P.O. Box 25087
Denver, CO 80225-0087)
Area served: CO, NM, UT, WY

Kansas City District Office
John Thorsky, director
11510 West 80th St.
Lenexa, KS 66214
Phone - (913) 752-2144
FAX - (913) 752-2136
(Mailing Address:
P.O. Box 15905
Lenexa, KS 66285-5905
Area served: IA, KS, MO, NE

Pacific region:
Oakland Regional Office
Mark Roh, director
Oakland Federal Building
1301 Clay St. Suite 1180 - N
Oakland, CA 94612-5217

Phone - (510) 637-3960
FAX - (510) 637-3976
Area served: AK, AZ, CA, HI, ID, MT, NV, OR, WA

Los Angeles District Office
Charles Breen, director
19701 Fairchild
Irvine, CA 92612-2506
Phone - (949) 608-2900
FAX - (949) 608-4498
Area served: AZ ,CA

Seattle District Office

Alonza E. Cruse, director
22201 23rd Dr. S.E.
Bothell, WA 98021
Phone - (425) 486-8788
FAX - (425) 483-4996
Area served: AK, ID, MT, OR, WA

San Francisco District Office
Barbara Cassens, director
1431 Harbor Bay Parkway
Alameda, CA 94502-7096
Phone - (510) 337-6700
FAX - (510) 337-6859
Area served: CA, HI, NV

Small Business Contacts in FDA's Centers

Center for Drug Evaluation and Research

CDER Small Business Assistance
(866)-405-5367
(301)-796-6707
CDERSmallBusiness@fda.hhs.gov
Office of Communications
Division of Drug Information
10001 New Hampshire Ave.
Rm 4147
Silver Spring, MD 20993

CDER Ombudsman
Virginia Behr
Telephone: 301-796-3436
E-mail: CDERombudsman@fda.hhs.gov

Small business assistance for drug firms can also be accessed at
http://www.fda.gov/smallbusinessdrugs

Center for Biologics Evaluation and Research

Manufacturers Assistance and Technical Training Branch (CBER)
(800) 835-4709
(301) 827-1800
Industry.Biologics@fda.hhs.gov
Division of Manufacturers Assistance and Training
Office of Communication, Outreach and Development
Food and Drug Administration
1401 Rockville Pike
Suite 200N/HFM-41
Rockville, MD 20852-1448

Additional contact information for CBER's Manufacturers Assistance and Technical Training Branch can be found on FDA's website at: http://www.fda.gov/BiologicsBloodVaccines/ResourcesforYou/Industry/default.htm.

CBER Ombudsman
Sheryl Lard Whiteford
Telephone: 301-827-0379
E-mail: Sherry.Lard@fda.hhs.gov

Center for Food Safety and Applied Nutrition

Outreach and Information Center (HFS-009)
1-888-SAFEFOOD
1-888-723-3366
industry@fda.gov
Center for Food Safety and Applied Nutrition
Food and Drug Administration
5100 Paint Branch Parkway
College Park, MD 20740

Center for Devices and Radiological Health

Division of Small Manufacturers, International and Consumer Assistance (DSMICA)
Food and Drug Administration
10903 New Hampshire Avenue
WO66 4613
Silver Spring, Maryland 20993
800-638-2041 or 301-796-7100 (Telephone)
301-847-8149 (Fax)
dsmica@fda.hhs.gov (Email)

DSMICA was mandated by the 1976 medical device legislation to provide technical and regulatory assistance to small manufacturers to help them comply with FDA requirements for medical devices.

More at http://www.fda.gov/MedicalDevices/DeviceRegulationandGuidance/ucm142656.htm

CDRH Ombudsman
David Buckles
Telephone: 301-796-5447
Fax: 301-847-8516
E-mail: CDRHOmbudsman@fda.hhs.gov

Center for Veterinary Medicine

240-276-9300
AskCVM@fda.hhs.gov
Communications Staff (CVM)
Food and Drug Administration
7519 Standish Place
HFV-12
Rockville, MD 20855

CVM Ombudsman
Marcia Larkins
Telephone: 240-276-9015
E-Mail: CVMombudsman@fda.hhs.gov

Center for Tobacco Products

1-877-CTP-1373
AskCTP@fda.hhs.gov
9200 Corporate Blvd.
Rockville, MD 20850

CTP Ombudsman
Les Weinstein
Telephone: 301-796-9239

Office of Small Business Assistance Website:
http://www.fda.gov/TobaccoProducts/ResourcesforYou/ForIndustry/ucm189635.htm
Office of Small Business Assistance E-mail Address:
Smallbiz.tobacco@fda.hhs.gov

Assistance for FDA's procurement and contract activities

FDA has a special program for seeking out and encouraging small companies to provide the Agency with needed supplies and services. For more information see the FDA Small Business Program website at http://www.fda.gov/AboutFDA/business/ucm134069.htm or contact:

Office of Small Disadvantaged Business Utilization
Small Business Specialist
Attn: Victoria Johnson
Food and Drug Administration
FHSL RM2037 HFA-500
5630 Fishers Lane
Rockville, MD 20857
Phone: (301) 827-1994
E-mail:Victoria.Johnson@fda.hhs.gov

Procurement activities include the purchase of scientific and laboratory equipment such as chemicals, glassware, furniture, electronic components, various species of laboratory animals, animal feed, bedding, holding cages, and other related supplies. FDA also solicits proposals and awards contracts for research, surveys and studies in the areas of management, construction/renovation, science, and medicine. The Agency has a specialist who is available to assist and counsel small companies in applying for the Agency's procurement and contracts.

Frequently called numbers and website index

FDA toll-free 888-INFO-FDA (888-463-6332)

Center for Biologics Evaluation and Research (CBER)

Consumer Affairs Branch
(800) 835-4709
(301) 827-1800
ocod@fda.hhs.gov

Division of Communication and Consumer Affairs
Office of Communication, Outreach and Development
Food and Drug Administration
1401 Rockville Pike
Suite 200N/HFM-47
Rockville, MD 20852-1448

Center for Devices and Radiological Health (CDRH)

1-800-638-2041 or 301-796-7100
Food and Drug Administration
10903 New Hampshire Avenue
WO66-4613
Silver Spring, MD 20993

Center for Drug Evaluation and Research (CDER)

Human Drug Information
(888) 463-6332
(301) 796-3400
druginfo@fda.hhs.gov
Division of Drug Information (CDER)
Office of Communications
10001 New Hampshire Ave.
Rm 4147
Silver Spring, MD 20993

Center for Food Safety and Applied Nutrition (CFSAN)

Outreach and Information Center (HFS-009)
1-888-SAFEFOOD
1-888-723-3366
Consumers: consumer@fda.gov
Industry: industry@fda.gov

Center for Food Safety and Applied Nutrition
Food and Drug Administration
5100 Paint Branch Parkway
College Park, MD 20740

Center for Veterinary Medicine

240-276-9300
AskCVM@fda.hhs.gov
Industry.AnimalVeterinary@fda.gov
Communications Staff (CVM)
Food and Drug Administration
7519 Standish Place
HFV-12
Rockville, MD 20855

National Institutes of Health (NIH)
Grant information line 301-451-0714, TTY 301-451-5936
http://grants.nih.gov/grants/oer.htm

Small Business Administration
http://www.sba.gov/ or 1-800-U-ASK-SBA (1-800-827-5722)

Government Printing Office
http://www.gpo.gov/ or 1-866-512-1800 or 202-512-1800

Helpful Information on the Internet

FDA

- Home page:
  http://www.fda.gov/ provides links to an expansive amount of regulatory and public health information and documents involving the Agency's activities.

- FDA-regulated industry:
  http://www.fda.gov/ForIndustry/ links to new information for regulated industry.

- Laws enforced by FDA:
  http://www.fda.gov/RegulatoryInformation/Legislation/ access to all FDA regulations.

- CitizenPetitions:
  http://www.fda.gov/RegulatoryInformation/Dockets/Comments/default.htm#petitions requests to add, remove, or change Agency regulations.

- FDA - Ombudsman:
  http://www.fda.gov/ForIndustry/DisputeResolution/ mediation, resolution of disputes with FDA and help for industry.

- Public Docket of Proposed Regulations:
  http://www.fda.gov/RegulatoryInformation/Dockets/ comment on proposed regulations, view pending regulations.

- Public Hearings:
  http://www.fda.gov/NewsEvents/MeetingsConferencesWorkshops/ how to participate in FDA's rulemaking process.

- Product recalls:
  http://www.fda.gov/Safety/Recalls/ product recall information, regulations, procedures.

- FOI - Handbook for requesting information and records:
  http://www.fda.gov/RegulatoryInformation/FOI/HowtoMakeaFOIARequest/ how to submit requests under the Freedom of Information Act.

- FDA Modernization Act:
  http://www.fda.gov/RegulatoryInformation/Legislation/FederalFoodDrugandCosmetic ActFDCAct/SignificantAmendmentstotheFDCAct/FDAMA/ changes to FDA regulations since 1997.

- Information for small and disadvantaged businesses wanting to do business with FDA:
  http://www.fda.gov/AboutFDA/business/ucm134069.htm

CBER

Standard operating policy and procedures:
- http://www.fda.gov/BiologicsBloodVaccines/GuidanceComplianceRegulatoryInformati on/ProceduresSOPPs/ license forms, instructions, guidance
- http://www.fda.gov/BiologicsBloodVaccines/ blood, biologic products, tissue, in-vitro diagnostics.

CDER
- Abbreviated New Drug Application (ANDA) application process (for generic drugs):
  http://www.fda.gov/Drugs/DevelopmentApprovalProcess/HowDrugsareDevelopedand Approved/ApprovalApplications/AbbreviatedNewDrugApplicationANDAGenerics/ forms for generic drug submissions, instructions, guidance.

- http://www.fda.gov/Drugs/ human drug products.

- http://www.fda.gov/Drugs/GuidanceComplianceRegulatoryInformation/DrugRegistrat ionandListing/ucm084014.htm facility registration and drug listing forms, instructions, guidance.

- IND application process:
  http://www.fda.gov/Drugs/DevelopmentApprovalProcess/HowDrugsareDevelopedand Approved/ApprovalApplications/InvestigationalNewDrugINDApplication/ investigational drug forms, instructions, guidance.

- New Drug Application (NDA) application process:
  http://www.fda.gov/Drugs/DevelopmentApprovalProcess/HowDrugsareDevelopedand Approved/ApprovalApplications/NewDrugApplicationNDA/ forms for new drug submissions, instructions, guidance.

- Assistance: http://www.fda.gov/smallbusinessdrugs assistance for new and small drug businesses.

CDRH

- http://www.fda.gov/MedicalDevices/ human and animal devices, in-vitro diagnostics, radiologicals, lasers.

- http://www.fda.gov/MedicalDevices/DeviceRegulationandGuidance/ device advice, search device databases; 510k / PMA help.

- http://www.fda.gov/MedicalDevices/DeviceRegulationandGuidance/HowtoMarketYourDevice/RegistrationandListing/ forms for facility registration and device listings, instructions, guidance.

- Assistance: http://www.fda.gov/MedicalDevices/DeviceRegulationandGuidance/ucm142656.htm assistance for small device businesses.

CFSAN

- http://www.fda.gov/Food/ features links to information about FDA-regulated food, dietary supplements, food additives, cosmetics, and dinnerware.

- Low Acid Canned Foods (LACF) / Acidified Food Registration / Process Filing: http://www.fda.gov/Food/FoodSafety/Product-SpecificInformation/AcidifiedLow-AcidCannedFoods/ forms for facility registration and filing a cooking process [acidified and low acid canned foods only], instructions, and guidance.

- Starting a Food Business: http://www.fda.gov/Food/ResourcesForYou/FoodIndustry/ information, assistance for new food businesses.

CVM

- http://www.fda.gov/AnimalVeterinary/ provides links to animal drugs, animal feed, pet products.

- FAQ's: http://www.fda.gov/AnimalVeterinary/SafetyHealth/FrequentlyAskedQuestions/ Questions and answers about veterinary regulations.

- New Animal Drug Application (NADA) /Abbreviated New Animal Drug Application (ANADA) application process (for generic animal drugs): http://www.fda.gov/AnimalVeterinary/DevelopmentApprovalProcess/NewAnimalDrugApplications/ forms for new animal drug submissions, instructions, guidance.

- Information about Animal Food and Feeds: http://www.fda.gov/AnimalVeterinary/Products/AnimalFoodFeeds/default.htm

- Information about the manufacture of pet food and pet treats:
  http://www.fda.gov/AnimalVeterinary/Products/AnimalFoodFeeds/PetFood/default.htm or
  http://www.fda.gov/AnimalVeterinary/NewsEvents/FDAVeterinarianNewsletter/ucm093741.htm

- Information about how FDA regulates veterinary devices:
  http://www.fda.gov/AnimalVeterinary/ResourcesforYou/ucm047117.htm

U.S. Government

- Superintendent of Documents:
  http://www.gpoaccess.gov/ access to all government publications.

- Code of Federal Regulations Online:
  http://www.gpoaccess.gov/cfr/ access to all government regulations that are online.

USDA

- Home page:
  http://www.usda.gov/ red meat, poultry regulations.

State health agencies

- http://www.fda.gov/ForFederalStateandLocalOfficials/
  FDA information for state agencies.